Developing A Progressively Productive Mindset

What to Do If You Are

Feeling Too Lazy

To Do Anything

Iyke Nwambie, DBA

Advancement Christian University, LLC

Copyright

Copyright © 2024 Dr. Iyke Nwambie

All rights reserved. All rights reserved. The characters and events portrayed in this book are fictitious. Any similarity to real persons, living or dead, is coincidental and not intended by the author. No part of this book may be reproduced, or stored in a retrieval system, or transmitted in any form or by any means, electronic, mechanical, photocopying, recording, or otherwise, without express written permission of the publisher.

ISBN: 9798323594962

Printed in the United States of America

Dedication

To all my teachers and students over the years, you have been the guiding lights and the inspiration behind this work. Your wisdom, curiosity, and dedication have shaped me as both a learner and a leader. This book is dedicated to you, with heartfelt gratitude for the lessons shared and the memories created.

Acknowledgment

I would like to express my deepest gratitude to my friends and family who have supported and encouraged me throughout this journey. Your love, understanding, and patience have been invaluable sources of strength and inspiration. This book is a reflection of our shared experiences and the unwavering belief you've had in me.

About The Author

Dr. Iyke Nwambie is a pharmacist, preacher, transformational speaker, and leadership advancement coach.

He helps regular people discover their places of authentic leadership and empowers leaders to advance their influences to become more authentic to themselves and maximize their profitability.

He is a firm believer in the idea that success and advancement are God's ideas for the human being instead of stagnation. He has been in personal, professional, business, spiritual, and leadership development for more than 25 years.

He has coached several thousands of entrepreneurs, leaders, pastors, students, and influencers to achieve their goals in the different areas of their lives.

He is the host of the Advancement Strategies Broadcast, Advance Your Leadership Broadcast and president of the Advancement Christian University.

Disclaimer

This book is not intended for application as a source of legal, business, accounting, or financial advice. All readers are advised to seek the services of licensed professionals in those fields. The contents of this book are based entirely on the personal experiences of the author. The author does not assume any responsibility or liability whatsoever for what you choose to do with this information. Apply your own judgment. Examples of past results in this book are solely for the purpose of illustration. No representation is made or implied that the reader will do as well from using any of the techniques

Other Books By Dr. Iyke Nwambie

1. Empowering The Stressed-Out CEO: 30 practical guides to managing stress and achieving success

2. Leadership Advancement Journal: How to stay inspired for high level productivity

3. Advancement Secrets: 10 Golden Secrets for Jumpstarting and Driving Your Business Dreams.

4. Unleash Your Inner Warrior with Faith Affirmations

5. God Will Enlarge Your Coast

6. Winning Mindset: How to stay positive even if everyone around you is thinking, talking, and acting negatively.

7. Keep Advancing: 170 Quotable Quotes for the Advancing Professional

8. Advanced Goal Setting: How to set goals for success even if you don't like setting goals.

9. Empowered Friendship: 7 Power Nuggets for Empowered Friendship

10. More Likable: Top 7 Ways to Make Yourself More Likable

11. Sharpen Your Leadership: Over 120 Winning Tips for Sharpening Your Thought Leadership.

12. S.M.I.L.E.: Transforming Sighs into Smiles: A Faith-Fueled Guide to Resilience, Purpose, and Joy in Life's Journey.

13. Mastering Self-Leadership: Your Personal Blueprint for High Performance and Advancement

14. Speak to Advance: Making Your Message Impactful in A Noisy World.

15. 366 Daily Advancement Devotional: How to keep advancing regardless of distractions.

16. The Young Leader

17. Productivity Hacks: 40 Ways to Supercharge Your Daily Routine and Get Things Done

Table of Contents

Introduction: The Dance of Desire and Diligence 11

Chapter 1: A General Overview of Mindset and Productivity.. 15

Chapter Two: Why Do We Sometimes Feel Lazy About Doing Anything?... 24

Chapter 3: Relevance of a Productive Mindset............. 27

Chapter 4: How I Learned to Empower My Mind for Productivity.. 32

Chapter 5: Why Every Thought Leader Needs a Productive Mindset... 35

Chapter 6: Using The F.L.O.U.R. Model To Activate A Productive Mindset If We Feel Lazy About Doing Anything 39

Chapter 7: How I Use the F.L.O.U.R. Model to Recalibrate My Enthusiasm When I Don't Feel Like Doing Anything 43

Chapter 8: Overcoming Overwhelm from Multitasking: A Story of Sarah and the F.L.O.U.R. Model 47

Chapter 9: Overcoming Information Overload and Burnout: A Story of Mark and the F.L.O.U.R. Model 51

Chapter 10: Finding Direction and Purpose: Alex's Journey with the F.L.O.U.R. Model 55

Chapter 11: Embracing Progress Over Perfection: Emily's Journey with the F.L.O.U.R. Model 59

Chapter 12: Finding Clarity and Direction: Ryan's Journey with the F.L.O.U.R. Model 63

Chapter 13: Achieving Work-Life Harmony: Sarah's Journey with the F.L.O.U.R. Model 67

Chapter 14: Recharging and Energizing: Mike's Journey with the F.L.O.U.R. Model 72

Chapter 15: Finding Recognition and Value: Lisa's Journey with the F.L.O.U.R. Model 76

Chapter 16: What Next? Embracing the F.L.O.U.R. Model for a Progressive Mindset 80

Conclusion 84

Appendix 88

12 Scriptural Affirmations for a Productively Progressive Mindset 88

Worksheets and Templates 90

12-Month Advancement Habit Tracker Template 91

Reflection Journal 93

12 Additional Tips and Techniques for the Productive Mindset 94

References 96

Introduction: The Dance of Desire and Diligence

Have you ever experienced that electrifying sensation after either delivering or listening to a transformative sermon, a keynote address, or even an impactful social media post or video on a Sunday afternoon?

That infectious enthusiasm that makes you feel unstoppable, ready to face Monday morning with unmatched passion and zeal? We've all been there, riding the wave of Sunday sermon inspiration into the promise of a productive week ahead.

Yet, as Monday morning dawns, that world-beating energy seems to have hit a snag, taking an unexpected hiatus. It's the age-old dilemma where Sunday's fervor meets the stark reality of Monday morning. This is the delicate dance between desire and diligence, a challenge faced by thought leaders like you who strive to maintain momentum and productivity throughout the week.

So, how do you keep that Sunday enthusiasm alive and translate it into consistent, diligent action throughout the week? It's time to master the art of balancing desire with discipline, turning inspiration into sustained productivity.

Welcome to the journey of cultivating a mindset where passion meets purpose, and enthusiasm fuels enduring success.

As an Advancement Coach, I've had the privilege of working with some truly remarkable leaders, influencers, pastors, and thought leaders. We've celebrated their victories, strategized their next moves, and yes, navigated the rollercoaster ride that is the dance between desire and diligence.

You see, it's not uncommon for our Sunday sermon highs to hit a bit of a snag come Monday morning. It's like our enthusiasm got stuck in traffic, and our motivation missed the memo about the workweek starting.

So, what gives?

Why does our enthusiasm sometimes disappear just when we need it most? Is there a secret conspiracy between Sunday sermons and Monday mornings that we're not aware of? Or perhaps our enthusiasm decided to take an impromptu vacation, leaving us to fend for ourselves in the daunting world of deadlines, to-do lists, and Monday morning meetings.

Well, fear not!

The dance of desire and diligence is a well-known routine, performed by leaders, influencers, pastors, authors, coaches, and yes, even Advancement Coaches like me.

It's a dance that requires rhythm, balance, and a healthy dose of humor (because let's face it, sometimes you just have to laugh at the absurdity of it all).

In this book, we'll explore the steps of this intricate dance, uncovering the science behind our Sunday sermon highs and Monday morning lows, and discovering practical strategies to maintain our enthusiasm and diligence throughout the week. We'll delve into real-life stories from those who've mastered the dance, and share insights, tips, and techniques that you can apply to your own life and leadership journey.

So, whether you're a pastor looking to inspire your congregation beyond Sunday morning, an influencer aiming to keep your audience engaged throughout the week, or a thought leader seeking to maintain momentum in your endeavors, this book is for you. Ready to perfect your dance moves and conquer the dance floor (and the workweek)? Let's dive in and embrace the dance of desire and diligence together!

Chapter 1: A General Overview of Mindset and Productivity

Do you know what could be responsible for that surge in enthusiasm on Sunday morning after a powerful sermon or keynote at a conference, only to find it waning by Monday mornings?

Often, this phenomenon is not just about fleeting motivation but is deeply rooted in how we operate our mindsets. Our mindset significantly influences our productivity and our ability to maintain momentum in pursuing our goals.

In this chapter, we'll delve into the foundational concepts of mindset and productivity, exploring how understanding and harnessing these elements can help us bridge the gap between Sunday's enthusiasm and Monday's action.

By cultivating a productive mindset and adopting effective productivity strategies, we can transform our aspirations into achievable goals and sustain our motivation throughout the week.

Let's embark on this journey to uncover the secrets of a productive mindset and lay the groundwork for consistent growth and success.

Understanding Mindset: Fixed vs. Growth

In my years as a pastor in Lagos, Nigeria, I had the privilege of witnessing incredible transformations among the members of our congregation. One such transformation was that of James (not real name), an early member of our church. When James first joined, he was hesitant and often doubted his abilities, particularly when it came to serving and leading others. He believed he had a Fixed Mindset, convinced that his skills and talents were limited and unchangeable.

Over time, with encouragement and support, James began to embrace a Growth Mindset. Inspired by the Apostle Paul's words in Philippians 4:13, "I can do all things through Christ who strengthens me," James started to see challenges as opportunities for growth and believed in his ability to develop new skills and overcome obstacles. This shift in mindset transformed James from a hesitant follower to a confident leader, illustrating the power of embracing a Growth Mindset.

Embracing a growth mindset doesn't happen overnight; it's a journey of continuous learning and self-discovery. Just like James, you too can begin to see challenges not as setbacks but as opportunities for growth. By adopting a growth mindset, you'll unlock your potential to develop new skills, overcome obstacles, and achieve greater success in your leadership journey.

Inspired by the groundbreaking work of Carol Dweck, who pioneered the concept of mindset in her seminal book "Mindset: The New Psychology of Success," adopting a growth mindset means seeing challenges not as setbacks but as opportunities for growth (Dweck, 2006).

Much like James, who shifted his perspective to view challenges as steppingstones rather than obstacles, you too can cultivate a mindset that embraces continuous learning and self-improvement. Dweck's research has shown that individuals with a growth mindset are more resilient, adaptable, and confident in their abilities to overcome obstacles and achieve success (Dweck, 2006).

Imagine approaching each day with a sense of curiosity and a willingness to learn from every experience, whether it's a triumphant victory or a challenging setback.

This shift in perspective empowers you to embrace change, adapt to new situations, and thrive in an ever-evolving landscape. As you cultivate a growth mindset, you'll find yourself growing more resilient, adaptable, and confident in your abilities to lead and inspire others.

So, are you ready to embrace the power of a growth mindset and unlock new levels of potential in your leadership journey? Let this be the catalyst that propels you forward, transforming challenges into steppingstones towards greater success and fulfillment.

The Science of Productivity

Now, let's talk about productivity. Imagine productivity as a garden. Just as a gardener carefully tends to their garden, planting seeds, watering plants, and removing weeds, a productive person diligently nurtures their tasks and goals.

James, once he embraced a Growth Mindset, began to approach his responsibilities with a gardener's mindset. He learned to prioritize tasks, allocate time efficiently, and eliminate distractions. Inspired by Stephen Covey's quote, "The key is not to prioritize what's on your schedule, but to schedule your priorities," James applied evidence-based productivity strategies like time blocking and the Pomodoro Technique to maximize his focus and efficiency.

According to a study by the University of California, Irvine, it takes an average of 23 minutes and 15 seconds to get back on track after a distraction. Armed with this statistic and a renewed focus, James became intentional about minimizing interruptions and optimizing his workflow, leading to a significant increase in his productivity.

The Role of Habits and Routines

As the saying goes, "We are what we repeatedly do. Excellence, then, is not an act, but a habit." James understood this principle well. He began to establish intentional habits and routines that supported his growth and productivity.

Drawing inspiration from Joshua 1:8, "Keep this Book of the Law always on your lips; meditate on it day and night," James implemented a morning routine of prayer and meditation on scripture, setting a positive and focused tone for his day. He also developed a habit of weekly planning sessions, where he would review his goals, prioritize tasks, and set intentions for the week ahead.

James's commitment to building intentional habits and routines played a crucial role in his transformation into a progressively productive person. He understood that productivity is not just about getting things done but about aligning his actions with his values and goals, day in and day out.

Productivity, Mindset, and a Productively Productive Person

To wrap up this chapter, let's define and describe productivity, a progressively productive mindset, and a progressively productive person.

Imagine a tree. The tree's roots represent our mindset, anchoring us and providing the foundation for growth. A Fixed Mindset keeps us rooted in limitations and doubts, while a Growth Mindset nourishes us with optimism and resilience.

The tree's trunk symbolizes productivity, supporting and connecting various branches (tasks and goals). Just as a tree needs sunlight, water, and nutrients to thrive, our productivity thrives on focus, discipline, and intentional effort.

Finally, the tree's branches represent a progressively productive person, reaching out and expanding towards the sky. A progressively productive person is not defined by perfection but by progress, continuously growing, learning, and adapting to new challenges and opportunities.

So, What is Productivity?

Productivity is the art of efficiently and effectively managing time, resources, and energy to accomplish specific goals or tasks. It involves prioritizing tasks, minimizing distractions, and optimizing workflows to achieve desired outcomes with the least amount of wasted effort.

What Is Mindset?

Mindset refers to the collection of beliefs, attitudes, and assumptions that shape our thoughts, behaviors, and responses to the world around us. It influences how we perceive challenges, approach opportunities, and interact with others. A growth-oriented mindset encourages resilience, adaptability, and a willingness to learn and grow, while a fixed mindset may limit our potential by viewing abilities as static and unchangeable.

Who Is the Productively Productive Person?

A productive person is someone who consistently achieves their goals by combining a growth-oriented mindset with effective productivity habits and strategies. They embrace challenges as opportunities for growth, maintain a positive attitude even in the face of setbacks, and continuously seek ways to optimize their performance and achieve meaningful results.

Chapter Two: Why Do We Sometimes Feel Lazy About Doing Anything?

Feeling lazy or unmotivated to do anything can stem from various factors, both psychological and physiological. Here are some common reasons why we might feel this way:

Lack of Clear Goals or Direction

Without clear goals or a sense of purpose, it's easy to feel unmotivated or unsure about what to do next. When we lack direction, tasks can feel overwhelming or pointless, leading to procrastination and feelings of laziness.

Mental Fatigue or Burnout

Constantly pushing ourselves without taking breaks can lead to mental fatigue or burnout. When our minds are tired, even simple tasks can feel challenging, and we may feel the need to rest or take a break.

Fear of Failure or Perfectionism

Fear of failure or a tendency towards perfectionism can also contribute to feelings of laziness. If we're afraid of making mistakes or not meeting our own high standards, we may avoid taking action altogether to protect ourselves from potential disappointment or criticism.

Lack of Energy or Physical Health Issues

Physical factors like poor sleep, nutrition, or underlying health issues can also impact our energy levels and motivation. If our bodies are not well-rested or nourished, we may feel lethargic and unmotivated to do anything.

Overwhelm or Information Overload

In today's fast-paced world, we're constantly bombarded with information and tasks competing for our attention. Feeling overwhelmed by the sheer volume of things to do can lead to paralysis and a sense of helplessness, making us feel lazy or unmotivated to start anything.

Understanding the underlying reasons behind our feelings of laziness or lack of motivation can help us address these issues more effectively and develop strategies to overcome them.

By identifying the root causes and implementing practical solutions, we can cultivate a productive mindset and regain our enthusiasm for pursuing our goals and responsibilities.

Chapter 3: Relevance of a Productive Mindset

In this chapter, we delve into the importance of cultivating a productive mindset and its profound impact on personal and professional growth.

The Impact on Personal and Professional Growth

Let's begin with the story of Tunde, a young entrepreneur I once coached. Tunde had a brilliant idea for a startup but often struggled with procrastination and self-doubt. One day, he shared with his frustration with me, saying, "I have so many ideas, but I just can't seem to take action on them."

I shared with Tunde the words of Tony Robbins, "The path to success is to take massive, determined action."

Inspired by this quote, Tunde began to cultivate a productive mindset. He started setting small, achievable goals for himself and celebrating his progress along the way. Over time, Tunde's business began to thrive, and he experienced significant personal and professional growth.

According to a study by the Harvard Business Review, individuals with a productive mindset are more likely to achieve their goals, experience career advancement, and report higher levels of job satisfaction. This underscores the importance of cultivating a productive mindset for both personal and professional success.

Overcoming Challenges and Obstacles

Now, let's turn to the story of David, a pastor I worked with who faced numerous challenges in leading his congregation. David often felt overwhelmed by his responsibilities and struggled to maintain motivation and enthusiasm.

I shared with David the story of Nehemiah from the Bible, who faced immense challenges in rebuilding the walls of Jerusalem but remained steadfast and focused on his goal.

Nehemiah 4:6 says, "So we rebuilt the wall till all of it reached half its height, for the people worked with all their heart." Inspired by this scripture, David began to approach his challenges with renewed determination and a productive mindset.

With this new perspective, David learned to break down his tasks into manageable steps, seek support from his community, and embrace setbacks as opportunities for growth. He discovered that a productive mindset not only helps us overcome obstacles but also empowers us to turn challenges into steppingstones towards success.

Enhancing Well-being and Satisfaction

Lastly, let's consider the story of Sarah, a knowledge worker who struggled with work-life balance and felt constantly stressed and overwhelmed. Sarah longed for a sense of well-being and satisfaction in her life but didn't know where to start.

I introduced Sarah to the concept of "work-life harmony" rather than "work-life balance," inspired by the quote from Arianna Huffington, "Success is not about climbing up the ladder, but about living a life you love." Sarah began to prioritize self-care, set boundaries, and make time for activities that brought her joy and fulfillment.

As Sarah cultivated a productive mindset, she found that she was not only more productive at work but also experienced improved well-being and greater satisfaction in all areas of her life. Research has shown that individuals with a productive mindset are more likely to experience lower levels of stress, better mental health, and overall higher levels of life satisfaction.

By developing a productive mindset, we can overcome procrastination, stay motivated, and achieve our goals, even when we don't feel like doing something.

As we continue this journey, remember the words of Proverbs 12:24, "Diligent hands will rule, but laziness ends in forced labor." With a productive mindset, we can cultivate diligence and enjoy the rewards of a life well-lived.

Chapter 4: How I Learned to Empower My Mind for Productivity

Have you ever noticed that your mind often defaults to negative thoughts or doubts?

According to Brian Tracy's insightful book, "Eat That Frog!: 21 Great Ways to Stop Procrastinating and Get More Done in Less Time" (Tracy, 2001), our minds have a natural tendency towards negativity, which can hinder our productivity and motivation.

However, by consciously activating positive thoughts and using the power of imagination, we can transform our mindset and enhance our productivity.

Personal Journey Towards Productivity

During a vacation where I had the chance to delve into Tracy's book, I was struck by the idea of using visualization as a tool for empowerment. Recognizing my own tendency towards negative thinking, I decided to harness the power of my imagination to envision and embrace the tasks I intended to accomplish. As I began to visualize and genuinely like what I intended to do, I found that taking action became easier and more enjoyable. This personal journey towards harnessing the power of visualization transformed my approach to productivity and ignited a renewed sense of enthusiasm for my goals.

Lessons Learned from Failures and Successes

Along this journey, I encountered both failures and successes that taught me valuable lessons about the importance of mindset and mental renewal. When I allowed negative thoughts to dominate, I noticed a significant dip in my motivation and productivity. However, by applying the visualization hack and actively renewing my mind through positive mental imagery, I experienced improved focus, increased motivation, and greater success in achieving my goals. These lessons taught me the profound impact our mindset has on our productivity and reinforced the importance of consciously choosing positive thoughts and beliefs.

Strategies and Techniques that Worked.

Drawing inspiration from the Bible verse Romans 12:2, which admonishes us to "be transformed by the renewal of your mind," I embraced the practice of mental renewal through visualization.

As a visually oriented person, creating mental pictures of my goals and tasks allowed me to connect with them on a deeper level and fueled my motivation to take action. Additionally, I adopted other productivity strategies and techniques, such as time blocking, goal setting, and prioritization, which complemented the visualization hack and further enhanced my productivity.

By combining the power of positive visualization with practical productivity techniques and the wisdom of Scripture, I learned to empower my mind for productivity and cultivate a mindset that supports my goals and aspirations.

This holistic approach to mental renewal and productivity has been instrumental in transforming my productivity journey and continues to serve as a foundation for achieving success in various areas of my life.

Chapter 5: Why Every Thought Leader Needs a Productive Mindset

I remember a conversation with a pharmacist colleague from our time in pharmacy school that has stuck with me over the years. I had challenged him about his productivity, noting that he was producing below what we considered his potential.

Initially offended, he later shared with me when we relocated to the USA more than 10 years after graduating from pharmacy school in Nigeria, how that conversation had spurred him to develop a productivity mindset that has since propelled him to greater success in his endeavors.

This transformation underscores the importance of a productive mindset, not just for individuals but especially for thought leaders who have the power to influence and inspire others.

The Importance of Role Modeling and Influence

As thought leaders, we often find ourselves in positions of influence, where our actions and attitudes can inspire others to strive for excellence. The story of my pharmacist colleague serves as a powerful reminder that our productivity and mindset can have a ripple effect, motivating others to develop their own productive habits. Proverbs 27:17 says, "Iron sharpens iron, and one man sharpens another." Just as iron sharpens iron, our commitment to productivity can sharpen and uplift those around us, creating a culture of excellence and growth.

Balancing Creativity and Discipline

Creativity and discipline are two sides of the same coin when it comes to thought leadership. While creativity fuels innovation and drives us to explore new possibilities, discipline ensures that we follow through on our ideas and turn them into tangible results. Albert Einstein once said, "Creativity is intelligence having fun," highlighting the importance of balancing our creative energies with disciplined action. By cultivating a productive mindset, we can harness our creativity effectively and channel it into meaningful projects that make a difference.

Leveraging Productivity for Innovation and Impact

Productivity is not just about getting things done; it's about maximizing our potential to create meaningful impact. According to a study by McKinsey & Company, organizations with a strong culture of productivity are 21% more likely to outperform their competitors. This statistic underscores the power of productivity in driving innovation and achieving sustainable success. As thought leaders, we have the opportunity to leverage our productivity to innovate in our fields and make a positive impact on the world around us.

Drawing inspiration from Matthew 25:23, "Well done, good and faithful servant; you have been faithful over a few things, I will make you ruler over many things," we are reminded of the importance of stewarding our time and talents wisely. By embracing a productive mindset, we can honor this call to stewardship and fulfill our potential to lead, innovate, and impact others.

As we continue on this journey of thought leadership, let us embrace the challenge of developing a productive mindset and harness its transformative power to inspire, innovate, and impact the world around us.

Chapter 6: Using The F.L.O.U.R. Model To Activate A Productive Mindset If We Feel Lazy About Doing Anything

"Do not wait to strike till the iron is hot; but make it hot by striking."

This insightful quote by William Butler Yeats reminds us that motivation is not always a prerequisite for action; sometimes, action itself can ignite motivation. If you find yourself generally unmotivated about wanting to do anything, you're not alone.

According to a survey by Gallup, only about 34% of U.S. workers are engaged at work, indicating a widespread issue of disengagement and lack of motivation.

F- Focus: Narrowing Down Priorities

The first step in activating a productive mindset is to focus on narrowing down priorities. As the saying goes, "You can do anything, but not everything." By identifying and focusing on the most important tasks or goals, we can avoid feeling overwhelmed and increase our motivation to take action. Research from the Journal of Experimental Psychology suggests that focusing on one task at a time can lead to increased productivity and better outcomes.

L- Limit Distractions: Creating a Distraction-Free Environment

Creating a distraction-free environment is crucial for maintaining focus and productivity. According to a study by the University of California, Irvine, it takes an average of 23 minutes and 15 seconds to get back on track after a distraction. By minimizing distractions and creating a conducive environment for work or study, we can optimize our concentration and motivation. Implementing strategies like turning off notifications, setting specific work hours, or using tools like the Pomodoro Technique can help limit distractions and boost productivity.

O- Organize: Planning and Scheduling

Planning and scheduling are essential components of a productive mindset. By organizing our tasks and allocating time for them, we create a roadmap that guides our actions and keeps us on track. The renowned thought leader Peter Drucker once said, "What gets measured gets managed." By setting clear goals, prioritizing tasks, and scheduling them effectively, we can manage our time more efficiently and increase our motivation to accomplish our objectives.

U- Unwind: Importance of Rest and Relaxation

Rest and relaxation are often overlooked but essential aspects of maintaining a productive mindset. Research from Harvard Business Review suggests that taking regular breaks and prioritizing self-care can lead to increased productivity, creativity, and overall well-being. By incorporating periods of rest and relaxation into our daily routines, we can recharge our energy levels, reduce stress, and enhance our motivation to tackle tasks with renewed vigor.

R- Reward: Celebrating Achievements and Milestones

Celebrating achievements and milestones along the way is a powerful motivator that reinforces positive behavior. According to a study by the Harvard Business School, acknowledging progress and celebrating small wins can boost motivation and lead to long-term success. By setting achievable goals and rewarding ourselves for reaching milestones, we can create a positive feedback loop that fuels our motivation and encourages continued progress.

As we implement these strategies and embrace the transformative power of the F.L.O.U.R. model, we can overcome inertia, ignite our motivation, and unlock our full potential for productivity and success.

Chapter 7: How I Use the F.L.O.U.R. Model to Recalibrate My Enthusiasm When I Don't Feel Like Doing Anything

Feeling stuck in a rut or lacking motivation happens to everyone, including thought leaders, speakers, authors, coaches, pastors, entrepreneurs, and professionals. When I find myself in such a situation, the F.L.O.U.R. model has been a game-changer in helping me recalibrate my enthusiasm and get back on track. One Bible verse that often inspires me during these times is Philippians 4:13, "I can do all things through Christ who strengthens me." This verse serves as a powerful reminder that with faith and determination, I can overcome challenges and achieve my goals, even when I feel unmotivated.

F- Focus: Narrowing Down Priorities

Identify One Priority: Instead of overwhelming myself with a long to-do list, I identify one priority or task that I want to accomplish.

Eliminate Distractions: I create a distraction-free environment by turning off notifications and setting a specific time to work on my chosen priority.

Set a Clear Goal: I set a clear and achievable goal for the task to provide direction and purpose.

L- Limit Distractions: Creating a Distraction-Free Environment

Minimize Digital Distractions: I put my phone on airplane mode or use apps to block distracting websites during work sessions.

Declutter Workspace: A tidy workspace helps declutter my mind. I spend a few minutes organizing my desk before starting.

O- Organize: Planning and Scheduling

Break It Down: I break down the chosen priority into smaller, manageable tasks or steps.

Time Blocking: I allocate specific time blocks on my calendar dedicated to working on the task.

Create a Checklist: A checklist helps me track my progress and provides a sense of accomplishment as I complete each item.

U- Unwind: Importance of Rest and Relaxation

Take Short Breaks: I incorporate short breaks between work sessions to rest and recharge.

Practice Mindfulness: I practice mindfulness or meditation for a few minutes to clear my mind and reduce stress.

R- Reward: Celebrating Achievements and Milestones

Celebrate Small Wins: After completing each task or reaching a milestone, I take a moment to celebrate and reward myself.

Reflect and Appreciate: At the end of the day or week, I reflect on what I've accomplished and appreciate my efforts, no matter how small.

The F.L.O.U.R. model serves as a practical and effective tool for recalibrating my enthusiasm and motivation when I don't feel like doing anything.

With the encouragement from Philippians 4:13, I am reminded of the strength and resilience that lies within me.

By focusing on narrowing down priorities, limiting distractions, organizing tasks, unwinding with rest and relaxation, and rewarding achievements, I can break through the inertia and reignite my passion for my work and goals.

This approach helps me maintain a productive mindset, stay motivated, and continue making progress towards my personal and professional aspirations.

Chapter 8: Overcoming Overwhelm from Multitasking: A Story of Sarah and the F.L.O.U.R. Model

Sarah, a successful entrepreneur and mother of two, found herself constantly overwhelmed by the demands of running her business while juggling her family responsibilities. She was often multitasking, trying to respond to emails, manage projects, attend meetings, and take care of her family, all at the same time. This constant juggling left her feeling exhausted, stressed, and unable to focus on any task effectively. It was during one particularly challenging week that Sarah turned to the F.L.O.U.R. model to help her overcome the overwhelm from multitasking.

F- Focus: Narrowing Down Priorities

Sarah realized that trying to do everything at once was not sustainable or productive. She decided to focus on prioritizing tasks by identifying the most important and urgent ones that required her immediate attention. She used the principle from Matthew 6:33, "But seek first the kingdom of God and his righteousness, and all these things will be added to you," to guide her in setting her priorities right. By aligning her tasks with her values and goals, Sarah was able to narrow down her focus and avoid the trap of multitasking.

L- Limit Distractions: Creating a Distraction-Free Environment

To limit distractions, Sarah turned off notifications on her phone and computer during work hours. She also set specific times for checking emails and messages, allowing her to concentrate fully on her prioritized tasks without constant interruptions. By creating a distraction-free environment, Sarah was able to maintain her focus and avoid getting sidetracked by non-urgent tasks or requests.

O- Organize: Planning and Scheduling

Sarah organized her tasks by breaking them down into smaller, manageable steps and scheduling them on her calendar. She allocated specific time blocks for working on each priority, ensuring that she had enough time to complete them without rushing. This systematic approach helped her stay organized and on track, reducing the overwhelm from multitasking.

U- Unwind: Importance of Rest and Relaxation

Recognizing the importance of rest and relaxation, Sarah incorporated short breaks between work sessions to rest and recharge. She used this time to take a walk, practice deep breathing exercises, or simply relax and clear her mind. By unwinding regularly, Sarah was able to maintain her energy levels and mental well-being, making it easier for her to tackle her tasks with renewed focus and enthusiasm.

R- Reward: Celebrating Achievements and Milestones

Finally, Sarah made it a point to celebrate her achievements and milestones along the way. After completing each priority or reaching a significant milestone, she took a moment to acknowledge her progress and reward herself. Whether it was treating herself to a favorite snack, taking a longer break, or simply patting herself on the back, these rewards helped boost her motivation and morale.

Through the F.L.O.U.R. model, Sarah was able to overcome the overwhelm from multitasking and regain control over her time and priorities. By focusing on narrowing down priorities, limiting distractions, organizing tasks, unwinding with short breaks, and rewarding herself for her achievements, Sarah created a balanced and sustainable approach to managing her responsibilities as an entrepreneur and mother. Her story serves as an inspiring example of how applying biblical principles and practical strategies can help us overcome challenges, achieve our goals, and live a more fulfilling and productive life.

Chapter 9: Overcoming Information Overload and Burnout: A Story of Mark and the F.L.O.U.R. Model

Mark, a devoted pastor and author, was overwhelmed by the constant influx of information from emails, social media, and various projects. This relentless stream of information left him feeling drained and on the verge of burnout. Searching for a solution, Mark turned to the F.L.O.U.R. model to help him regain control over his time and energy.

F- Focus: Setting Boundaries for Information Consumption

To regain control, Mark started by focusing on setting boundaries for information consumption. He unsubscribed from unnecessary emails, muted non-essential notifications, and designated specific times to check emails or social media. Inspired by Romans 12:2, "Do not be conformed to this world, but be transformed by the renewal of your mind," Mark aimed to renew his mind with meaningful and edifying content, filtering out unnecessary distractions.

L- Limit Distractions: Organizing Workload and Prioritizing

Next, Mark aimed to limit distractions by organizing his workload. He created a structured schedule with designated times for checking emails, social media, and news updates. By prioritizing his tasks and focusing on what truly mattered, Mark was able to manage his time more effectively and reduce distractions.

O- Organize: Structuring Time and Tasks

Mark recognized the need to organize his time and tasks more efficiently. He allocated specific time slots for different activities, ensuring he had dedicated time for work, rest, and relaxation. This structured approach allowed him to stay focused and productive without feeling overwhelmed by the demands of his responsibilities.

U- Unwind: Disconnecting and Relaxing

Understanding the importance of rest and relaxation, Mark prioritized time to unwind and disconnect from work. He spent quality time with his family, engaged in hobbies he enjoyed, and practiced mindfulness and meditation. By taking time to rest and recharge, Mark was able to reduce stress and prevent burnout.

R- Reward: Celebrating Achievements and Expressing Gratitude

Finally, Mark practiced rewarding himself by celebrating his achievements and expressing gratitude. After completing tasks or reaching milestones, he took a moment to acknowledge his progress and thank God for His guidance and provision. This practice of gratitude and celebration helped maintain Mark's positive mindset and boost his morale.

Through the F.L.O.U.R. model, Mark successfully overcame information overload and burnout by Focusing on setting boundaries, Limiting distractions through organization, Organizing his time and tasks, taking time to Unwind and relax, and Rewarding himself for his achievements. By integrating biblical principles with practical strategies, Mark was able to create a balanced and sustainable approach to managing his responsibilities as a pastor and author. His story serves as an inspiring example of how intentional living, discipline, and faith can help us navigate the challenges of modern life and maintain a healthy work-life balance.

Chapter 10: Finding Direction and Purpose: Alex's Journey with the F.L.O.U.R. Model

Alex, a passionate speaker and coach, found himself feeling lost and lacking clear direction in his professional life. He was juggling multiple projects and responsibilities but felt like he was going in circles without a clear sense of purpose or goals. Feeling stuck, Alex turned to the F.L.O.U.R. model to help him find clarity and direction.

F- Focus: Defining Clear Goals and Priorities

Alex began by focusing on defining clear goals and priorities. Inspired by Habakkuk 2:2, "Then the Lord answered me and said: 'Write the vision and make it plain on tablets, that he may run who reads it,'" Alex took time to reflect on his vision and purpose. He identified his core values, passions, and long-term objectives to create a clear roadmap for his professional journey.

L- Limit Distractions: Organizing Tasks and Setting Boundaries

To limit distractions and stay on track, Alex organized his tasks and created a structured plan to guide his actions. He broke down his goals into smaller, manageable steps and allocated specific time frames to work on each task. By setting boundaries and focusing on his priorities, Alex was able to reduce distractions and stay focused on his path.

O- Organize: Creating a Roadmap and Action Plan

With clear goals in place, Alex organized his thoughts and ideas to create a detailed roadmap and action plan. He mapped out the steps needed to achieve his goals, identified potential challenges, and developed strategies to overcome them. This structured approach gave Alex a clear direction and helped him stay organized and proactive.

U- Unwind: Celebrating Achievements and Reflecting

Recognizing the importance of rest and reflection, Alex took time to unwind and celebrate his achievements along the way. After reaching significant milestones, he rewarded himself by taking a break, enjoying a hobby, or spending quality time with loved ones. These moments of rest and celebration helped Alex maintain motivation and momentum.

R- Reward: Maintaining Motivation and Momentum

Finally, Alex practiced rewarding himself for achieving milestones to maintain his motivation and momentum. Whether it was treating himself to a favorite meal, taking a day off, or simply acknowledging his progress, these rewards kept Alex inspired and motivated to continue pursuing his goals.

Through the F.L.O.U.R. model, Alex was able to overcome his lack of clear goals and direction by Focusing on defining his purpose, Limiting distractions through organization, Organizing his tasks with a detailed roadmap, taking time to Unwind and reflect, and Rewarding himself for his achievements. By integrating biblical principles with practical strategies, Alex found the clarity and direction he was seeking in his professional life. His story serves as an inspiring example of how intentional goal-setting, organization, and self-care can help us find purpose, stay focused, and achieve success in our endeavors.

Chapter 11: Embracing Progress Over Perfection: Emily's Journey with the F.L.O.U.R. Model

Emily, a talented artist and designer, struggled with perfectionism and a fear of failure that often paralyzed her creativity and progress. She would spend countless hours over-analyzing her work, striving for perfection, and fearing the judgment of others. Feeling trapped by these self-imposed expectations, Emily turned to the F.L.O.U.R. model to help her break free from the cycle of perfectionism and fear of failure.

F- Focus: Prioritizing Progress Over Perfection

Emily began by focusing on progress over perfection, inspired by Philippians 3:13-14, "Brothers and sisters, I do not consider myself yet to have taken hold of it. But one thing I do: Forgetting what is behind and straining toward what is ahead, I press on toward the goal to win the prize for which God has called me heavenward in Christ Jesus."

She reminded herself that it's okay to make mistakes and that progress is more important than perfection.

L- Limit Distractions: Avoiding Over-Analysis and Decision-Making Paralysis

To limit distractions and avoid over-analysis, Emily made a conscious effort to stay focused on her work without getting bogged down by minor details or second-guessing her decisions. She learned to trust her instincts and embrace the creative process, letting go of the need for everything to be perfect.

O- Organize: Setting Realistic Goals and Deadlines

Emily organized her tasks by setting realistic goals and deadlines for her projects. Instead of aiming for perfection, she focused on completing her work to the best of her ability within the given timeframe. This approach helped her stay on track and avoid the procrastination that often accompanies fear of failure.

U- Unwind: Rewarding Action Over Outcome

Recognizing the importance of celebrating small victories, Emily rewarded herself for taking action, regardless of the outcome. Whether it was completing a project, trying out a new technique, or receiving positive feedback from clients, Emily took time to acknowledge her efforts and celebrate her progress.

R- Reward: Embracing Growth and Learning

Finally, Emily practiced rewarding herself by embracing the growth and learning that comes from taking action and making mistakes. She adopted a growth mindset, viewing failures and setbacks as opportunities to learn and improve, rather than as reflections of her worth or abilities.

Through the F.L.O.U.R. model, Emily was able to overcome her perfectionism and fear of failure by Focusing on progress over perfection, Limiting distractions and avoiding over-analysis, Organizing her tasks with realistic goals and deadlines, Unwinding by rewarding action over outcome, and Rewarding herself by embracing growth and learning. By integrating biblical principles with practical strategies, Emily found the courage to break free from the cycle of perfectionism and embrace the creative process with confidence and joy. Her story serves as an inspiring example of how embracing progress over perfection, setting realistic goals, and celebrating small victories can lead to personal growth, creativity, and fulfillment.

Chapter 12: Finding Clarity and Direction: Ryan's Journey with the F.L.O.U.R. Model

Ryan, a young entrepreneur, found himself feeling overwhelmed and directionless in his professional life. He had many ideas and ambitions but lacked clear goals and a sense of direction to guide his actions. Feeling stuck and frustrated, Ryan turned to the F.L.O.U.R. model to help him find clarity and purpose.

F- Focus: Defining Clear Goals and Priorities

Ryan began by focusing on defining clear goals and priorities. Inspired by Proverbs 16:9, "In their hearts humans plan their course, but the Lord establishes their steps," Ryan spent time reflecting on his vision and values. He identified his core aspirations, both short-term and long-term, to create a clear roadmap for his entrepreneurial journey.

L- Limit Distractions: Organizing Tasks and Setting Boundaries

To limit distractions and stay focused on his goals, Ryan organized his tasks and set boundaries for his time and energy. He broke down his goals into smaller, manageable steps and allocated specific time slots to work on each task. By setting boundaries and focusing on his priorities, Ryan was able to reduce distractions and stay on track.

O- Organize: Creating a Roadmap and Action Plan

With clear goals in place, Ryan organized his thoughts and ideas to create a detailed roadmap and action plan. He mapped out the steps needed to achieve his goals, identified potential challenges, and developed strategies to overcome them. This structured approach gave Ryan a clear direction and helped him stay organized and proactive.

U- Unwind: Celebrating Achievements and Reflecting

Recognizing the importance of rest and reflection, Ryan took time to unwind and celebrate his achievements along the way. After reaching significant milestones, he rewarded himself by taking a break, enjoying a hobby, or spending quality time with loved ones. These moments of rest and celebration helped Ryan maintain motivation and momentum.

R- Reward: Maintaining Motivation and Momentum

Finally, Ryan practiced rewarding himself for achieving milestones to maintain his motivation and momentum. Whether it was treating himself to a favorite meal, taking a day off, or simply acknowledging his progress, these rewards kept Ryan inspired and motivated to continue pursuing his goals.

Through the F.L.O.U.R. model, Ryan was able to overcome his lack of clear goals and direction by

Focusing on defining his purpose, Limiting distractions through organization, Organizing his tasks with a detailed roadmap, taking time to Unwind and reflect, and Rewarding himself for his achievements. By integrating biblical principles with practical strategies, Ryan found the clarity and direction he was seeking in his entrepreneurial journey. His story serves as an inspiring example of how intentional goal-setting, organization, and self-care can help us find purpose, stay focused, and achieve success in our endeavors.

Chapter 13: Achieving Work-Life Harmony: Sarah's Journey with the F.L.O.U.R. Model

Sarah, a dedicated professional in the corporate world, found herself constantly overwhelmed by her demanding job, often sacrificing her personal time and well-being for the sake of work. She struggled with poor work-life balance, feeling stressed, exhausted, and disconnected from her loved ones. Feeling burnt out and unhappy, Sarah turned to the F.L.O.U.R. model to help her achieve a healthier balance between her work and personal life.

F- Focus: Prioritizing Self-Care and Well-being

Sarah began by focusing on prioritizing self-care and well-being, inspired by 3 John 1:2, "Beloved, I pray that all may go well with you and that you may be in good health, as it goes well with your soul." She realized that taking care of herself was crucial for her overall well-being and happiness. Sarah committed to making self-care a priority, whether it was getting enough sleep, eating healthily, or engaging in activities that nourished her soul.

L- Limit Distractions: Setting Boundaries Between Work and Personal Life

To limit distractions and maintain a healthy work-life balance, Sarah organized her schedule to include specific times for work, rest, and personal activities. She set clear boundaries between her work and personal life, avoiding the temptation to check work emails or take calls during her personal time. By setting boundaries, Sarah was able to focus on the present moment and fully engage in her personal life without the constant intrusion of work-related stressors.

O- Organize: Scheduling Time for Rest and Relaxation

Sarah organized her schedule to include time for rest, relaxation, and activities that brought her joy and fulfillment. She blocked out specific time slots for exercise, hobbies, and spending quality time with loved ones. This structured approach helped Sarah maintain a healthy balance between her work and personal life, allowing her to recharge and rejuvenate outside of work hours.

U- Unwind: Prioritizing Activities That Bring Joy and Fulfillment

Recognizing the importance of rest and relaxation, Sarah prioritized activities that brought her joy and fulfillment. Whether it was taking a nature walk, reading a book, or enjoying a hobby, Sarah made time to unwind and disconnect from work. These moments of relaxation helped Sarah reduce stress, improve her mood, and enhance her overall well-being.

R- Reward: Celebrating Small Wins and Achievements

Finally, Sarah practiced rewarding herself by celebrating small wins and achievements along the way. After successfully maintaining a healthier work-life balance for a week or reaching a personal milestone, she rewarded herself with something she enjoyed, whether it was a spa day, a movie night, or a special treat. These rewards served as positive reinforcement and motivated Sarah to continue prioritizing her well-being and work-life harmony.

Through the F.L.O.U.R. model, Sarah was able to overcome poor work-life balance by Focusing on self-care and well-being, Limiting distractions through boundary-setting, Organizing her schedule to include time for rest and relaxation, Unwinding with activities that brought joy and fulfillment, and Rewarding herself for her achievements.

By integrating biblical principles with practical strategies, Sarah achieved a healthier balance between her work and personal life, leading to improved well-being, happiness, and fulfillment.

Her story serves as an inspiring example of how intentional self-care, boundary-setting, and prioritizing well-being can lead to a more harmonious and fulfilling life.

Chapter 14: Recharging and Energizing: Mike's Journey with the F.L.O.U.R. Model

Mike, a hardworking software engineer, found himself constantly battling physical fatigue and a lack of energy. His demanding job, coupled with long hours of sitting and staring at a computer screen, took a toll on his health and well-being. Feeling drained and exhausted, Mike turned to the F.L.O.U.R. model to help him combat physical fatigue and boost his energy levels.

F- Focus: Prioritizing Rest, Sleep, and Relaxation

Mike began by focusing on prioritizing rest, sleep, and relaxation, inspired by Psalm 127:2, "It is in vain that you rise up early and go late to rest, eating the bread of anxious toil; for he gives to his beloved sleep." He realized the importance of getting adequate restorative sleep and taking breaks throughout the day to recharge. Mike committed to setting a consistent sleep schedule and incorporating relaxation techniques, such as deep breathing and meditation, into his daily routine.

L- Limit Distractions: Maintaining a Healthy Work Environment

To limit distractions and create a conducive work environment, Mike organized his workspace to promote better ergonomics and reduce physical strain. He invested in an ergonomic chair, adjusted the height of his computer monitor, and positioned his keyboard and mouse to minimize strain on his wrists and shoulders. By maintaining a healthy work environment, Mike was able to focus better and reduce physical fatigue.

O- Organize: Scheduling Regular Breaks and Physical Activity

Mike organized his day to include regular breaks and physical activity. He set reminders to take short breaks every hour to stretch, walk around, and rest his eyes. Additionally, Mike scheduled time for physical activity, such as going for a walk during lunch breaks or doing simple exercises at home. These breaks and physical activities helped rejuvenate his body and boost his energy levels.

U- Unwind: Practicing Relaxation Techniques

Recognizing the importance of relaxation, Mike practiced relaxation techniques to unwind and reduce stress. He incorporated deep breathing exercises, mindfulness meditation, and progressive muscle relaxation into his daily routine to help him relax and recharge. These relaxation techniques helped Mike manage stress more effectively and improve his overall well-being.

R- Reward: Celebrating Small Achievements and Progress

Finally, Mike practiced rewarding himself by celebrating small achievements and progress. Whether it was sticking to his sleep schedule for a week, taking regular breaks, or incorporating physical activity into his daily routine, Mike rewarded himself with something he enjoyed, such as watching his favorite movie, enjoying a hobby, or treating himself to a healthy snack. These rewards served as positive reinforcement and motivated Mike to continue prioritizing his health and well-being.

Through the F.L.O.U.R. model, Mike was able to combat physical fatigue and lack of energy by Focusing on rest, sleep, and relaxation, Limiting distractions through a healthy work environment, Organizing his day to include regular breaks and physical activity, Unwinding with relaxation techniques, and Rewarding himself for his achievements. By integrating biblical principles with practical strategies, Mike improved his physical well-being, energy levels, and overall quality of life. His story serves as an inspiring example of how intentional self-care, ergonomic practices, and regular physical activity can help combat physical fatigue and boost energy levels.

Chapter 15: Finding Recognition and Value: Lisa's Journey with the F.L.O.U.R. Model

Lisa, a talented graphic designer, often felt overlooked and underappreciated in her workplace. Despite her hard work, creativity, and dedication, she struggled with a lack of recognition and reward for her contributions. This lack of acknowledgment left her feeling demotivated and unfulfilled. Seeking a solution, Lisa turned to the F.L.O.U.R. model to help her find ways to appreciate her own achievements and derive satisfaction from her work.

F- Focus: Recognizing the Value of Her Work

Lisa began by focusing on recognizing the intrinsic value of her work, inspired by Colossians 3:23-24, "Whatever you do, work at it with all your heart, as working for the Lord, not for human masters, since you know that you will receive an inheritance from the Lord as a reward. It is the Lord Christ you are serving." She reminded herself that her work had a purpose and that she was making a valuable contribution, not just to her employer but also to the people who benefited from her designs.

L- Limit Distractions: Setting Regular Checkpoints for Reflection

To limit distractions and stay focused on her goals, Lisa organized her tasks to include regular checkpoints for reflection and celebration of progress. She set short-term and long-term goals and marked them on her calendar. Whenever she achieved a milestone, no matter how small, she took a moment to reflect on her progress and celebrate her achievements.

O- Organize: Planning Celebrations and Rewards

Lisa organized her tasks to include planning celebrations and rewards for herself. Whether it was treating herself to a nice meal, buying a new art supply, or taking a day off to relax, Lisa made sure to reward herself for her hard work and accomplishments. These rewards served as positive reinforcement and helped boost her morale and motivation.

U- Unwind: Focusing on Positive Impact and Value

Recognizing the importance of maintaining motivation and enthusiasm, Lisa practiced unwinding by focusing on the positive impact of her work and the value it brought to others. She collected feedback from clients and users who appreciated her designs, which reminded her of the significance of her contributions and fueled her passion for her work.

R- Reward: Celebrating Achievements and Milestones

Finally, Lisa practiced rewarding herself by celebrating her achievements and milestones. After reaching a goal or completing a project, she took time to acknowledge her hard work and treat herself to something special.

These rewards served as a source of motivation and encouragement, helping Lisa stay motivated and focused on her goals.

Through the F.L.O.U.R. model, Lisa was able to handle the lack of recognition and reward by Focusing on the value of her work, Limiting distractions through regular checkpoints for reflection, Organizing celebrations and rewards, Unwinding by focusing on the positive impact of her work, and Rewarding herself for her achievements. By integrating biblical principles with practical strategies, Lisa found ways to appreciate her own contributions, stay motivated, and derive satisfaction from her work. Her story serves as an inspiring example of how self-recognition, goal-setting, and positive reinforcement can help combat feelings of underappreciation and boost motivation and morale.

Chapter 16: What Next? Embracing the F.L.O.U.R. Model for a Progressive Mindset

As we've journeyed with our protagonists—Mike, Sarah, Ryan, and Lisa—we've witnessed their transformations using the F.L.O.U.R. model to overcome various challenges. Now, you might be wondering, how can you apply these principles to your own life to generate a progressively productive mindset?

Maintaining Momentum and Consistency

Maintaining momentum and consistency is vital for long-term success. Zig Ziglar once said, "People often say that motivation doesn't last. Well, neither does bathing —

that's why we recommend it daily." Just like our protagonists, you can implement the F.L.O.U.R. model as a daily practice. Focus on prioritizing tasks, limiting distractions, and rewarding yourself regularly. Draw inspiration from Philippians 4:13, "I can do all things through Christ who strengthens me," reminding yourself that with faith and consistency, you can achieve your goals.

Adapting to Changes and Challenges

Life is full of changes and challenges, and learning to adapt and grow through them is crucial. Embrace a growth mindset and draw inspiration from James 1:2-4, "Consider it pure joy, my brothers and sisters, whenever you face trials of many kinds, because you know that the testing of your faith produces perseverance. Let perseverance finish its work so that you may be mature and complete, not lacking anything." Focus on what you can control and adapt to the rest. Remember, 85% of the things people worry about never happen, so don't let fear hold you back.

Continuing Growth and Development

Continuing growth and development are key to personal and professional fulfillment. Commit to lifelong learning and draw wisdom from various sources. Read books by thought leaders like Brené Brown and seek guidance from preachers and spiritual leaders who remind you of the importance of faith, perseverance, and staying connected to your purpose. Embrace the metaphor of a tree, which grows steadily over time, drawing nourishment from its roots and adapting to its environment.

The Journey Continues

As you continue your journey, remember the metaphor of a marathon, not a sprint. Pace yourself, stay focused on your goals, and celebrate each milestone along the way. Success is not a one-time event but a series of small, consistent efforts over time.

Embrace the F.L.O.U.R. Model for Your Journey

The F.L.O.U.R. model is a powerful tool that can help you cultivate a progressively productive mindset, enabling you to overcome the feeling of not wanting to be productive when you should be doing something. By focusing on F - Focus, L - Limit Distractions, O - Organize, U - Unwind, and R - Reward, you can create a balanced and fulfilling life.

Remember, the journey to a progressively productive mindset is a marathon, not a sprint. It requires dedication, resilience, and a willingness to adapt and grow. But with the F.L.O.U.R. model as your guide and the wisdom of thought leaders, preachers, and motivational speakers to inspire you, you are well-equipped to face whatever challenges lie ahead.

So, why wait? Embrace the F.L.O.U.R. model today and start cultivating a progressively productive mindset that will empower you to live a balanced, fulfilling, and purpose-driven life. Your journey to overcoming procrastination and embracing productivity starts now!

Conclusion

As we wrap up our exploration of the F.L.O.U.R. model and its transformative power, let's recap the key insights and strategies that can help you cultivate a productive mindset. We've journeyed with our protagonists—Mike, Sarah, Ryan, and Lisa—as they navigated various challenges and embraced the F.L.O.U.R. model to overcome procrastination and generate a progressively productive mindset. Now, let's reflect on what we've learned and look ahead to the journey that lies before you.

Recap of Key Insights and Strategies

Maintaining Momentum and Consistency: Zig Ziglar's wisdom reminds us that motivation, like bathing, is something we should do daily. By implementing the

F.L.O.U.R. model as a daily practice, focusing on prioritizing tasks, limiting distractions, and rewarding yourself regularly, you can maintain momentum and consistency in your journey.

Adapting to Changes and Challenges: Embracing a growth mindset, as inspired by James 1:2-4, allows you to adapt and grow through life's changes and challenges. Focus on what you can control, and don't let fear hold you back from pursuing your goals.

Continuing Growth and Development: Commit to lifelong learning and draw wisdom from various sources. Whether it's reading books by thought leaders like Brené Brown or seeking guidance from spiritual leaders, continuing growth and development are key to personal and professional fulfillment.

Embracing the F.L.O.U.R. Model: The F.L.O.U.R. model—F - Focus, L - Limit Distractions, O - Organize, U - Unwind, and R - Reward—serves as a powerful tool to help you cultivate a progressively productive mindset and overcome procrastination.

Final Thoughts on Cultivating a Productive Mindset

Cultivating a productive mindset is not a destination but a journey—a journey that requires dedication, resilience, and a willingness to adapt and grow. As you embrace the principles of the F.L.O.U.R. model and draw inspiration from thought leaders, preachers, and motivational speakers, remember that success is a continuous process of growth and self-discovery.

Encouragement for the Journey Ahead

As you embark on your journey to cultivate a progressively productive mindset, know that you are not alone. With the F.L.O.U.R. model as your guide and the support of a community of like-minded individuals, you have everything you need to succeed. Embrace the challenges, celebrate the victories, and remember that every step you take brings you closer to your goals.

So, why wait? Start your journey today, embrace the F.L.O.U.R. model, and cultivate a progressively productive mindset that will empower you to live a balanced, fulfilling, and purpose-driven life. Your journey to overcoming procrastination and embracing productivity starts now!

Appendix

12 Scriptural Affirmations for a Progressively Productive Mindset

1. I can do all things through Christ who strengthens me. *(Philippians 4:13)*

2. I consider it pure joy when I face trials because they produce perseverance. *(James 1:2-4)*

3. I commit my plans to the Lord, and He establishes them. *(Proverbs 16:3)*

4. God has plans for my welfare, future, and hope. *(Jeremiah 29:11)*

5. I am transformed by the renewal of my mind, not conformed to this world. *(Romans 12:2)*

6. I am not afraid, for God is with me; He strengthens and upholds me. *(Isaiah 41:10)*

7. I work heartily for the Lord, not for men. *(Colossians 3:23-24)*

8. I commit my way to the Lord and trust in Him. *(Psalm 37:5)*

9. I seek first the kingdom of God, and all things are added to me. *(Matthew 6:33)*

10. I run with endurance the race set before me, laying aside every weight. *(Hebrews 12:1)*

11. I am created for good works and walk in them. *(Ephesians 2:10)*

12. I have a spirit of power, love, and self-control, not fear. *(2 Timothy 1:7)*

Worksheets and Templates

F.L.O.U.R. Model Worksheet

F - Focus: _____

L - Limit Distractions: _____

O - Organize: _____

U - Unwind: _____

R - Reward: _____

12-Month Advancement Habit Tracker Template

Habit:
_____

Month/Week	Jan	Feb	Mar	Apr	May	Jun	Jul	Aug	Sep	Oct	Nov	Dec
Week 1	☐	☐	☐	☐	☐	☐	☐	☐	☐	☐	☐	☐
Week 2	☐	☐	☐	☐	☐	☐	☐	☐	☐	☐	☐	☐
Week 3	☐	☐	☐	☐	☐	☐	☐	☐	☐	☐	☐	☐
Week 4	☐	☐	☐	☐	☐	☐	☐	☐	☐	☐	☐	☐

Instructions:

1. **Habit:** Write down the habit you want to track in the space provided at the top.
2. **Months/Weeks:** Fill in the months or weeks for the year across the top row.
3. **Weeks:** Fill in the weeks for each month in the first column.

4. **Tracking:** Use a symbol (☐ or ✔) to indicate whether you completed the habit for each day/week.
5. **Review:** At the end of each month, review your progress to see how consistently you've practiced your habit.

Feel free to customize this template to fit your specific habits and tracking preferences. This habit tracker can be a valuable tool in your journey to cultivate a growth mindset and develop new habits that support your personal and professional growth.

Reflection Journal

Date: _____

Today's Wins:
_____
_____

What I Learned Today:
_____
_____

Gratitude for Today:
_____
_____

12 Additional Tips and Techniques for the Productive Mindset

1. **Time Blocking**: Allocate specific blocks of time for different tasks.

2. **Pomodoro Technique**: Work in short bursts followed by a 5-minute break.

3. **Digital Detox**: Take regular breaks from electronic devices.

4. **Mindfulness Meditation**: Practice mindfulness to improve focus.

5. **Physical Activity**: Incorporate regular physical activity into your routine.

6. **Healthy Eating**: Maintain a balanced diet.

7. **Hydration**: Drink plenty of water throughout the day.

8. **Quality Sleep**: Prioritize sleep with a regular schedule.

9. **Accountability Partner**: Find someone to keep you on track.

10. **Continuous Learning**: Invest in personal development.
11. **Gratitude Practice**: Cultivate daily gratitude.
12. **Limit Multitasking**: Focus on one task at a time.

Feel free to print and use these worksheets and templates to help you implement the F.L.O.U.R. model and cultivate a progressively productive mindset.

Remember, these affirmations, resources, and tips are here to guide and support you on your journey to overcoming procrastination and embracing productivity.

References

Cirillo, F. (2006). The Pomodoro Technique: The life-changing time-management system. Cirillo Company.

Covey, S. R. (1989). The 7 habits of highly effective people: Powerful lessons in personal change. Simon & Schuster.

Dweck, C. S. (2006). Mindset: The new psychology of success. Random House.

Holy Bible, New International Version. (1984).

Tracy, B. (2001). Eat That Frog!: 21 Great Ways to Stop Procrastinating and Get More Done in Less Time. Berrett-Koehler Publishers.

University of California, Irvine. (2018). The high cost of interruptions.

www.ingramcontent.com/pod-product-compliance
Lightning Source LLC
Chambersburg PA
CBHW071102240526
45471CB00016B/2399